look for yellow

anna barroso

Look for Yellow
Hues of the Heart Collection (Book 1)
© 2024 Solar Stories
All rights reserved.

Cover Image: Anna Barroso
Cover Design: Anna Barroso
Formatting: Anna Barroso
Proofreading: Chelsey Gordon

Printed in the U.S.A.
First Edition: June 2023
Second Edition: November 2024
Paperback ISBN: 979-8-9918962-3-8
E-book ISBN: 979-8-9918962-4-5

Anna Barroso
www.solar-stories.com

look for yellow

hues of the heart
book 1

anna barroso

to the ones who are like me,
broken but redeemed

for the weeper
for the dreamer
for the reader

for the weeper

ONE: you are what you eat

has your heart ever hurt so much that even after your eyes become heavy, your heart still pumps out of your chest so quickly that your brain scrambles to make sense of it? and you're left with a plate full of eggs with a side of bacon and fruit. food for thought.

has your tongue ever been wounded so badly that no antidote can cure the venom dripping from your teeth? and you're left in your self-pity because you bit your tooth instead of biting your lip, causing your body to rot.

TWO: gorilla glue
I struggle to put down a book
I struggle to pick one up
I fight to get lost in my head
I fight to find my way back
I long to be alone
I long for the days I'm not lonely
I'm trapped inside a body I do not know
I'm tapped inside a word that won't show

THREE: teach me to be brave
I'm scared
of life
of this
of me
      help

FOUR: hazy
depression
is an everyday
journey without
everyday results
2pm laughing with your friends
or
2 days later alone on the couch

FIVE: the thief among me
dressed like a nightmare
slithering in through a window
looting the rooms
the last piece of the puzzle
infinite hallways
lost in a maze
leaving behind no mistakes
unable to wake
from the nightmare

SIX: show and tell
I hate all your shows. I see what's behind your pretty face and your long eyelashes. I hear the lies you tell people. I hear the screaming that your fingers make as they cross one more time. I can tell that you're immune to breaking hearts. I see your smile as they shatter. glass shards and your paper heart.

I hate all your shows. I hate that you tell people that you're happy. I see how you hurt others because when you finally give your heart away, they give their souls away. you demon. you steal souls like you breathe. slowly and then all at once. slowly you walk away on eggshells as you hold your breath. careful now, we wouldn't want you to drown in your broken dreams. stop overanalyzing what's not really there.

I hate all your shows. stop lying to yourself. you can't break what's fixed. fixed. fixed in time. heartbreak. ticktock. call time. time to pretend. time to act. time to run lines and rehearse your monologue. you're selfish. stop thinking about yourself. you're not the only one hurting. the world shouldn't stop because you couldn't blink that tear away.

I hate all your shows. I hate the sound of your heart dropping and spilling all over the floor. stop waiting for someone to just know that you're broken. they'll believe the lies that you tell, but you never will. curtain call. take a bow. standing ovation. you've fooled them once again. but that's all acting really is, isn't it?

SEVEN: forbidden fruit
she lay alone in a bed meant for two
she lay alone and
wanted only to see the one
she loved most
her stomach eating away
at her flesh from the inside out
a consuming fire
a fire
flames licking her back
flames licking her scars
she waits around for him
to
come back

EIGHT: childhood dreams
all around they're
laughing and playing
and swaying you think
just for a second
how nice
it would be
to just smile
and to get off
the teeter-totter
you're riding

NINE: little atlas
I feel like I'm living in the shadows. and I can't prove myself, no matter how hard I try. I'm locked in a box with walls built by you. each day, you slide a picture through the cracks, an image of what you want me to be. a murderous action. for if I try to be who you want me to be, the walls will collapse in on me. but it's also my only chance of freedom. I want to fly away, but I have no wings.
will I forever be locked in this never-ending maze?

TEN: sleepwalking
I'm not afraid of
dying
I'm afraid of
gaining
a thousand friends
upon my departure

where were you
when I was alive?

ELEVEN: she stands for nothing
she sat alone in a crowded room. wondering if anyone felt as alone as she did. wanting someone to reach out to her. instead, she just sits and waits. waiting for the bell to ring to leave. waiting to be noticed.

she is waiting until the day that she will not dread going to that class. the class. remove the suffix and split the prefix. the cell. locked away in a prison of abandonment and selfishness. nobody wants to leave their comfort zone. the cell. division. divide and conquer. conquer your fears. she sits alone, afraid to make the first move. justifying her thoughts. if they cannot face their fears, why should she? we are advancing all the time. how come we have no courage? technology makes our life easier. so why is it so hard to speak in person?

she sits and listens. she listens to all the conversations that she will never be a part of. listens to music to try and drown out the voices. listens to try and look unapproachable because that is how she feels. listens because she would rather listen to something she controls, than something someone else controls. in a world that spins one thousand miles per hour, everything moves so slowly. paradox. hypocrites.
she sits and waits and listens and contributes to all the things she complains about as she writes it all down on her cell phone screen.

TWELVE: I promise, your life matters
I want to run away, so I can breathe. it's suffocating. this skin is squeezing me so tightly that I don't know which way is up. it's crippling, this guilt inside me. I'm ashamed to even look at myself. I can't let anyone near me. I can't let anyone hear me. I thought for a split-second that I could do it. that I could be enough. the thought will lurk in my mind forever. the feeling of betraying the people you love most. I can't be trusted. leave me! for your own good, leave. every inch of me itches with regret. I can't crawl away quick enough. I can't shrink down small enough. I can't do anything right. I'm useless. I'm helpless. I'm pathetic. don't look at me! I can't hold your stare. every fiber of this wretched body can't deteriorate fast enough. I just want out. unlock this cage that I'm drowning in!

    I'm sorry

THIRTEEN: self-diagnosed claustrophobia
I can't breathe
this box is getting smaller
I just want to be free
but I'm trapped by myself

I built these walls
but I cannot break them
I'm trapped by others' opinions
this and that. what's right?

I don't know what to think
this world is screaming at me
I'm screaming at me
leave me alone! let me be!

FOURTEEN: treasure hunt
do you ever feel like you push people away because you have no choice? I'm guilty of fighting those who want to get close to me. I'm so toxic. I don't want to poison those around me. I don't want to blind those who look at me.

I'm a paradox. I love to be alone, but I hate being lonely. I hate being alone with my thoughts. it's so easy to be reminded of all the pain I try to hide. so many chambers and so many locked doors. so many secrets and so many scars.
I'm not even sure that I know all the bones hidden away. so many years of covering it them up. so many years of smiling through rotten teeth. I'm without a compass or a map, lost in my head.

FIFTEEN: to the ones who didn't get to say goodbye
the earth mourned for you
this morning
yesterday
you were gone without warning
today
was full of shattered showers
I already miss you
but I refuse to bring you flowers
you're worth more than clichés

I fell numb
when I got the call
the ground hard and wet
from the rainfall
soaking as I watch the world turn
gray skies blanketed my soul
I'll never stop
telling the story of ol'
you'll live on within me

petrichor, a sweet aroma
water up to my ears
climbing to my nose
covered in all my tears
I'm not fighting it
not caring when
or where I am
and then
      black

and suddenly
i feel the water wash away
and i hear a whisper say
"it wasn't supposed to be this way"
peace crashes over me
steadying my ceased   heartbeat
He holds out His hand
and then i'm on my feet
standing under a canopy of green

hand in hand, we walk
strolling on streets of gold
stopping to smell the roses
and to harvest the marigold
He turns and says,
"this is My perfect design"
and joy fills my soul
"I'll come back for you in no time"
so patiently i'll wait

with a newfound wisdom
i know what i'm to do
i will stand with courage
and love those scarred in black and blue
because i have tasted the honey
and i've drank from the well
to share my story
of my rescue from hell
and of Him in
      white

SIXTEEN: not a breakup
why did you drop me like I didn't matter?
why did you replace me like I was never there?
don't you remember all the times we laughed together?
can you recall all the times we cried together?
you left me alone
and I'm angry
I can't believe you don't see what you've done
I don't know what to do

SEVENTEEN: ticktock
created and man-made, holding lives in the hands and dictating sorrows and joys. slow and steady, never-ending, eternal, but never enough. capturing moments on squares smeared with ink. the hands never letting go.

grandfathers stand tall and watch as the owl makes her best. she sings lullabies to her children, as they lay to rest. restful days and restless nights. blankets covering those who rest peacefully. the hands placing flowers at their bedside.

standing on a log amongst the swallowing waters, the hands beckon to cross the cavern. the owl and her children soaring high above. with lifeless lungs and barely a grasp reaching for the hands as they stretch across. standing tall and looking grandfather in the face.

EIGHTEEN: sink or swim
I'm lost in a pattern of too little or too much. a chaotic continuum. I want to feel wanted. I'm drowning in self-pity, but I refuse to grab the lifeboat.

NINETEEN: ghosting
it falls over me when you're not around
my joy is nowhere to be found
you're my sweet sensation
my motivation
your smile shines through the dark
your life makes its mark
your touch sends me away
I'm at peace for the day
your lips soothe the pain
but what do I have to gain?
it will never last
repetition of the past
my life repeats
and you'll retreat
after all, who wants to love me?
I'm worth nothing, you see
so back to my coma I go
into my little world that I know

TWENTY: playtime puppeteer
I used to move for you
to bend for you
to touch you
but you were wrong for me

now I'm stuck with
the pain of these memories
not because I miss you
but because you broke me

TWENTY-ONE: beauty from ashes
I'm constantly losing my soul
in different places
sometimes I'm careless with
those who caress my heart
I'm no fool, though
only one boy holds it

girls, they're the problem
you see, something is wrong with me
I can easily produce a list
of all the silent breakups that occurred
bullet insults deep in my heart
poison promises in my gut

I'm not good at making friends
I don't know how to hold onto them
was my grip too tight?
did I strangle you?
or was it too loose?
and you fell through the cracks?

sometimes I still get angry
at all of you
for dumping me
without remorse
for replacing me
without mourning

but in reality
you've made me who I am
I don't know if I have
the strength to thank you
but
I'm beginning to like who I am now

TWENTY-TWO: the cry of an introvert
I think best on paper
I like the way it feels
to know something is there
and to touch something real
it clears my mind
of all the secrets I'm keeping
and of all the whispers I find
but I noticed there's no one here
and I feel free
because I have nothing to fear
it's good to be alone
but watch out for lonely
it's a quick and deadly cancer
to be with you and you only

TWENTY-THREE: lol thx anxiety
what if I don't go through with it?
what if it's all a mystery to you?
what if it just becomes a lost dream for me?
what would I do?
would I mourn it or just accept it?

TWENTY-FOUR: what's a panic attack like?
it begins in the mind. it's planted and takes root. quickly like a weed, but quietly like grass. thorns sprout and the poison's released. causing the body to convulse. weeping. hyperventilating. dying. the heart beats out of the chest, because impending doom awaits. the world collapses in and your body is crushed. limp, you lay there blankly. no thoughts. no breathing. no movement. just lost in time and space, somewhere floating. looking down and hanging on by a few threads. get up and carry yourself like a balloon. and that's how you get through the days

TWENTY-FIVE: I miss you more than I can think about
what do I do about you?
I don't know if I need to
be angry or sad
or both
what do I do now that
you're not here
that you left without a goodbye
that
      that
              you're go--
what do I do?

TWENTY-SIX: don't ruin me by assuming me
they say confidence is attractive
but how am I supposed to be
if I'm still accused of being sixteen?
when people ask what high school I go to
while I'm a college graduate
how am I supposed to like how I look
when everyone assumes I'm less
while they treat me like I'm a rebellious teen
trying to dress to impress the older guys
while I'm just trying to dress my age
how am I supposed to think I'm pretty
when they say I look childish
"looking young now, will be good later"
but what if my "prime" never comes?
how about you just stop assuming who I am
because everyone knows what happens when you assume
except it's not me, it's only u
I'm tired of it
I'm over it
to me, looking young will always be old.

TWENTY-SEVEN: dropping like flies
I think about dying often
not because I want to
but because I'm used to it

TWENTY-EIGHT: what do I do with these bones?
my lungs are black
from breathing you in
my heart is blue
from holding you too long
my soul is gray
because you stripped it away

TWENTY-NINE: He clothes the wildflowers
I may think that you're all right, but inside there's a fight. I may think it's all okay, but could it be your last day? does anyone know? can anyone tell? that inside you're only thinking about how good death can be? an escape from reality. an escape from your worst fears. an escape from torture. a way back to the people who were taken from you. a way back to warm arms that you haven't felt in so long. and then you ask, "do I even remember what they feel like?" you miss them too much. left or right, up or down. you're blinded by the pain. the saying "love them to death" becomes too real for you. are you cursed? no. well, not entirely. you've allowed yourself to grow so numb. numb to words, numb to touch, numb to you.

frail and pure, saturated by love and blood, like a rose. thorns skirt around you. they grew as a barrier, a cage for your heart. but I see you. I know you. I love you. I gave you these thorns, not as a weapon, but as a tool. I know you feel alone, unwanted, and lost. but I'm here. I've found you and I want to take you home.

for the dreamer

ONE: joy
joy
      joy
            joy
full of it
and longing
for joy
to return quickly
joy while
slowly dying
is just
joy while
continually smiling
joy in pain
pain without gain
is just life
without joy

just
      sunflower
            searching

TWO: happiness
forehead kisses
four black paws
forever family
for real friends

THREE: tower tales
locked
in a tower
possibly a
princess
probably a
prisoner
trapped
in chains
without a
key
without knowing
knowledge is
power
knowledge is
key
without caring
because the
tower is all she
knows

FOUR: magic wand
sunflowers are gifts
of sunshine
you can hold in your hand
wave them like a wand
to make the
nighttime
disappear

FIVE: homesick
i long to join You
i'm confused
it's complicated to express
i'm thankful for Your abundant giving
i don't want this to end
but i crave to be with You
i can't have both at the same time
      and it scares me

SIX: chosen
looking for successes while only wearing dresses, used to making messes. always stuck in my mind, just trying to find the next line to get me out. hooked and caught on the whole lot that's wrong with me. who am i gonna be? who's gonna like what they see? wandering through crowds of nothing and no one. just wanted to have fun, but now i'm done, looking at the gun in my hand.
then i heard You

i heard You

i heard You from out of the blue, didn't know what to do. but it's not really blue, it's boldly yellow. and the world slows and i'm mellow because Your sweet voice, like a cello, is calling my name. and i'm going insane looking at the man who was slain before me. i'm seeing sunshine for the first time and it's divine. who am iI that You named me, that You saved me, that You love me?

SEVEN: head in the stars
I walk around headless
unaware of my thoughts
the spiral staircase
narrow and rocky
keep the balance
or I'll fall right into
the black hole
of my past

EIGHT: where am I now?
of all the people I've ever lost
I've mourned for myself the most

NINE: US-1
I want more
ride the airwaves
outside my car
type of days

TEN: quartering
am I a result of
who I want to be
or who others want
sometimes I don't know

I'm crippled by
the desire to please others
maybe then they'd stay

ELEVEN: Your rod and Your staff comfort me
You are constant
i am temporary
i used to run to You
my comfort
my redemption
those where the early days
the golden days
i hate that i
push and pull
You
are so good
You
are so forgiving
You
are so loving
i
am so wretched
i
am so
so
    so
lost with
You

TWELVE: can I just be a cute watering can?
I often hate the way that I am. I hate how I can never speak my mind. I hate that I can't make up my mind. how is it possible that I feel so lost in something that is made for me? something that is me. desiring to sprinkle flowers but soaking them into a puddle. longing to float in a serene pool of wisdom, but often drowning in a tsunami of confusion. struggling to take breaths, to rise above the storm, but just settling on the stone-cold bottom. it's dark and it's heavy. where do I go from here?

THIRTEEN: phd in lonely
isn't it funny
how school doesn't always teach
what you need to know?
how to file taxes
how to balance a checkbook
why there are letters in math

how to make friends

FOURTEEN: reminisce
I used to shine
when I saw you

FIFTEEN: prone to wander
thick black anger is raging
just like a dull, dark storm outside the front door
she doesn't think the Son will come out; it's been ages
the darkness eats her alive

finally, her walls come down
seven years of marching on, and she sees the light
emotions, they stir, and become one big blur
happiness, she could not find

seven people came with plagues
she saw a sea of glass with fire inside
"where were You when i was so alone here?"
seven bowls of wrath on earth

"are You coming to take me home?"
seeing dead rise from their graves and standing before the throne
the storm is easing up now; she can see
"behold, I have come again"

SIXTEEN: what is truth?
moments come
memories go
along with
perspective

is it right?

SEVENTEEN: in His image
life is a canvas
the painters are many
actions create the picture
mistakes are made
forgiveness is the eraser
the colors blend
and lines overlap
history repeats
and heartache adds
friends are each a different color
some are faint
while others are prevalent
the brushstrokes narrate the story
the deep, the pain
the light, the love
each is unique
and created at once

EIGHTEEN: smile big
the prettiest smile
is the one of pure joy
a toy in the hands of a child
a groom as the bride floats down an aisle
a father playing air guitar in the car

NINETEEN: thank you, sunshowers
I love the rain
the smell as it cleanses the earth
the way that it dances on the pavement
the sound of it smacking on the patio

but

I love the sunshine
the way it tans his skin
the warm hugs it shares
the way it brightens a room

I love when
they live together in harmony
taking turns to make flowers grow
creating puddles for jumping

TWENTY: let it shape you, not define you
hello and goodbye
I don't always know how to interact with my past
but I'm thankful for the memories
I appreciate you
but I don't miss you
it's best to move forward
but I wanted to say
      thank you for it all

TWENTY-ONE: wildflowers in a vase
I love putting flowers
in my shortalls
because it makes me
feel wild
      but tame

TWENTY-TWO: sprinkles on ice cream
I want to save the gray skies
keep them in a jar
so that the world will cry when I can't
I want to pocket the raindrops
so that I can listen to the sound
when I'm alone

TWENTY-THREE: just breathe
breathing is a beautiful thing
calm and contemplative
sustaining and saturated
real and restful
invisible and imaginary
panicked and poised
mighty and manageable
vital and violent
what does it mean?

TWENTY-FOUR: ode to a dream
when I was little
I wanted to be a
tap-dancing
singing
astronaut

I don't know how to
tap dance, sing
and I'm definitely not an astronaut

TWENTY-FIVE: and more precious than jewels
she's happy and beautiful
with the sun in her eyes
and the Son in her soul

TWENTY-SIX: peasant pleas
King of grace
show Your face
and do not allow
them to vow
a life without You

TWENTY-SEVEN: hemisphere hunting
my mind is a meadow
   with never-ending flowers
   a place where
   my ideas thrive
   and my thoughts are whole
my mind is a coop
   clipped wings stunt flight
   crabgrass slicing my feet
   a place where
   anxiety thrives
   my fears are whole

TWENTY-EIGHT: i surrender
i remember
life without You
the barren
  empty
  desert
the consuming
  destructive
  black hole
i remember
fighting but never winning

TWENTY-NINE: leave the ninety-nine
You are so beautiful
i am so unworthy
You are so loving
      i am so betraying
You keep me whole
      i push You away
You chase after me
      i spit in Your face
You'll never stop pursuing me
      i can come home

THIRTY: Known
from darkness to light
    dust to death
    flood to drought
    twelve to one

You were there

for the reader

ONE: sealed with a kiss
please be gentle with my words
I may look like I have it all together
but my heart is paper-thin

TWO: xoxo, me
I only saw her eyes
but it was enough
to see the hurt
the heartbreak
and the beautiful

so much strength
and courage
she's wounded from
so many battles

keep fighting,
little warrior

THREE: photosynthesize
it's okay for some days to be spent in bed
but remember to open the windows
and let the sunlight in
breathe in the fresh air
tomorrow's a fresh start

FOUR: a letter to my sixteen-year-old self
I wish that that I wasn't afraid to say what I really think to people. I'm not a liar, if that's what you're thinking. I was recently complimented by a friend because she thinks I'm "courageous." It took me off guard. I'm a coward. I can't speak my mind. I'm not afraid of doing "scary" stuff like talking to a stranger or eating lunch with someone who sits by themselves. But the thought of telling someone your true thoughts, that's courage. I'm not fake. I don't pretend to "like" anyone, because there's no one that I don't like (well, except maybe a few teachers). I just want to express myself.

dear little caterpillar. you were so young. you thought you knew everything. darling, there are scarier things to come. but with each fear, comes something spectacular. maybe now, conversations with strangers may make you uncomfortable, but that's okay. dear little caterpillar, your cocoon is almost finished now. the world is scary but coming outside is so brave. each day is a victory. with each flight, your bravery will grow. do not fear, because you are loved.

just, little caterpillar, just remember to stop and smell the roses.

FIVE: to the ones who pushed me
hey there, little artist
this is an ode to you
you've made me who I am
thank you for shaping me
for molding me
for igniting a fire in me
you see, I wouldn't be me
without you
so, thank you for it all

SIX: this is real, and this is me
here I sit
in a café
where we used to be
in a town
that doesn't know us anymore
I try to drown my feelings
with this pen
something so relaxing
causes so much anxiety
I can't deny it anymore

SEVEN: petrichor
I like to cry in the shower
because I'll never know
how many tears I've shed
and it makes the pain manageable

EIGHT: take deep breaths, little duck
the sight of red
flowing from my arms
will never leave my sight
the shiv in my hand
the look of defeat
crushed by my onus
longing for the feeling of something
or anything
just to breathe
and know that I'm alive
count to three
one – inhale
two – hold
three – live

NINE: liar, you told me that you'd be fine
you are so much braver than I
here you sit
words in your hands
and you breathe freely
not pressured to make something beautiful
out of your ugly reality

TEN: they're my gift to you
these words have
stained my lips
they're tattooed on my heart
they're not much
and not the best
but they're mine

ELEVEN: your life is precious
of all the words
my pen will say
these may be some
of the most important

TWELVE: orphan come home
to the ones who
lost a loved one
        fell into a bad habit
        tripped over your tongue
        can't seem to find their way
        are is paralyzed while slipping away
to the one who
        hates their thoughts
        feels betrayed by their body
        can't seem to succeed
        doesn't want to wake up tomorrow
I see you and I love you

THIRTEEN: when I compare myself
I feel
suppressed, torn down, knocked and beaten
bruised, mocked, scorned, and weakened

FOURTEEN: the pungent paradox
tell me that you care
but don't let it go to my head
show me that you notice
but don't let me stand out
appreciate my works
but please don't compare me

FIFTEEN: it kills me that I can't
I feel most alive
when I sing

SIXTEEN: leeward
my mind is the deepest ocean
my words are a puddle
neither reflecting
what I mean

SEVENTEEN: rumination
a haiku for you
I think I'm pretty funny
but they don't get it

EIGHTEEN: please be nurturing with them
maybe it's the name
or the tune in my head
but I'll have to agree
because in this, my soul has bled
for this book is mine and I'm proud
but "these words are my diary
screaming out loud"

ode to Anna Nalick's "Breathe (2AM)"

NINETEEN: oxymoron
I want to be beautiful
sometimes, it's all I think about
I want to be known
  and noticed
  and loved
but I don't want the spotlight

I'm addicted to authenticity
still, I can't help but push you away
  because I can't let you see the real me
call me a hypocrite if you please
it'll just prove that everyone leaves

I need to be original
  but everything's already been done
It's a perilous plight
  and a captivating catastrophe

TWENTY: silent but deadly
silent tears
aren't welcomed
nor dismissed
they are
intimate
and I know them well

TWENTY-ONE: tame it
your words are either
a drug
or a poison

TWENTY-TWO: look for yellow
yellow days
happy gaze
mellow daze
unfortunate graze

blue weeks
tortured freaks
absolutely weak
steady peak

yellow times
blue chimes
slightly shine
dutifully mine

Acknowledgments

First and foremost, I need to thank my God and my King. He is the Creator of all things and therefore created me. It is because of Him that I write. Thank you, Christ, for the gift of salvation–it is because of You that I have life. Thank you, Spirit, for guiding me and teaching me. It is because of You that this collection was written. You've convicted me time and time again to share it.

Erick, Mom, and Dad. I wouldn't be a writer if it wasn't for your continual encouragement. Thank you.

Thank you for my early readers. Thank you for those who read and reviewed the first edition of look for yellow.

Soli Deo gloria.

More by Anna Barroso

Ash Learns to Roll (The Adventures of Ash, Book 1)

Seas the Day (coming January 2025)

Subscribe to her newsletter.

www.ingramcontent.com/pod-product-compliance
Lightning Source LLC
Chambersburg PA
CBHW051348040426
42453CB00007B/463